The Gift for All People

The
G·I·F·T
for All People

MAX LUCADO

Multnomah® Publishers *Sisters, Oregon*

THE GIFT FOR ALL PEOPLE
published by Multnomah Publishers, Inc.

© 1999 by Max Lucado
International Standard Book Number:
1-59052-342-3
1-59052-439-X

Compiled and edited by Karen Hill
Cover design by UDG DesignWorks, Inc.
Cover Image by PixelWorks Studio
Christmas Edition cover by Photodisc

Much of the content of this book is taken from previously published works.
A complete list of references can be found in the back of the book.

Multnomah is a trademark of Multnomah Publishers, Inc.,
and is registered in the U.S. Patent and Trademark Office.
The colophon is a trademark of Multnomah Publishers, Inc.

Printed in the United States of America

For information:
MULTNOMAH PUBLISHERS, INC.
POST OFFICE BOX 1720
SISTERS, OREGON 97759

Library of Congress Cataloging-in-Publication Data

Lucado, Max.
    The gift for all people / Max Lucado.
        p.   cm.
    Includes bibliographical references.
    ISBN 1-57673-464-1 (alk. paper)
    1-59052-342-3
    1-59052-439-X
    1. Devotional literature, English. 2. Jesus Christ—Devotional
literature.   I. Title.
BV4832.2.L77 1999
242—dc21   98–31656
                                                            CIP

05 06 07 08 09 10 — 21 20 19 18 17

✦

Dedicated to all missionaries around the world.

How beautiful are the feet of those who bring good news.

ROMANS 10:15

CONTENTS

The Gift of a Savior

Ransom for Sinners

Bounteous Grace

The Choice

PROLOGUE

✦

*B*right future" said it all. Single, good looking, recent college grad. His family loved him, girls noticed him, career opportunities invited him.

And yet, while Eric appeared confident without, he was tormented within. Tormented by inner voices he could not quiet. Tortured by mental images he could not avoid and by thoughts he could not understand. So, desperate to escape the torment, Eric decided to escape from life. On a gray, rainy February day, Eric walked out the back door of his home. He never returned.

When Eric walked away, someone was watching. His sister Debbie saw her brother leave, his tall frame ambling down the street. She assumed he would return. He didn't. She hoped he would call. He didn't. She thought she could find him. She couldn't. Hours became years. Years of wandering and wondering.

As Eric wandered, Debbie wondered. Where could he be? What could have happened? Is he all right? Is he alive?

Where Eric journeyed, only God and Eric know. But we know that he ended up thousands of miles from his home. And somewhere along his path, somehow, Eric began to believe he had been given an assignment. Someone noticed Eric going through a dumpster, looking for food. And that someone suggested Eric sweep up in exchange for the garbage. Eric interpreted this comment as an assignment: He believed he had been given a permanent commission to clean up a roadside in San Antonio, Texas.

To the local residents, Eric's lanky form and bearded face became a familiar feature as he walked up and down his "assigned" section of Interstate 10, gathering trash. Through the years many tried to assist him, but Eric resisted. He was content to survive on what he collected. He created a home out of a hole in a vacant lot. He designed a wardrobe out of split trousers and a torn sweatshirt. Summer sun was deflected by an old hat, winter chill softened by a plastic bag covering his shoulders.

His weathered skin and stooped shoulders made him look twice his forty-four years. But then, sixteen years living on the side of the road would do that to you.

It had been sixteen years since Debbie had seen her brother. And she might never have seen him again, had it not been for two events. The first was the construction of a car lot on top of Eric's hovel. The second was a pain in Eric's abdomen. The car lot took Eric's shelter. The pain took Eric's health.

When EMS found Eric curled in a ball on the roadside, he was already dying of cancer. Another few months and Eric would be gone. And with no known family or relatives, he would die as he'd lived—alone.

Eric's court-appointed temporary guardian couldn't handle this thought. *Surely someone is looking for this man,* reasoned the attorney. So the attorney searched the Internet for anyone missing a brown-haired adult male with Eric's last name.

A reply came from a New Hampshire woman. Could this homeless man in Texas be the brother she'd been seeking for so long? The description seemed to match, but she had to know for sure. So Debbie, her husband, and two children headed for Texas.

By the time Debbie arrived, Eric had been released from the hospital. Debbie found him near his old home, resting against the side of a building. One look was all it took to convince her— the search was over. She saw beyond the sun-dried skin, beneath the unkempt hair and beard. She saw her brother.

Eric, however, didn't recognize his sister. The years had ravaged his mind. Debbie longed to embrace this long-lost sibling, but her instincts told her she must await his cue.

And then something small led the way. Eric noticed an angel pin Debbie was wearing. He was intrigued by it. When Debbie offered the pin to Eric, he said yes. He even allowed her to pin the angel on his shirt. And with that one gesture, she, at long last, touched her brother.

Debbie came to Texas planning to spend a week. But a week passed and she couldn't leave. She rented an apartment, began homeschooling her children and reaching out to her brother. It wasn't easy. He didn't always recognize her. He wouldn't call her by name. One day he cursed her. He refused to sleep in her apartment. He didn't want her food. He didn't want to talk. He just wanted his vacant lot. He wanted his "job."

But Debbie didn't give up on Eric. Weeks became months, and still the sister stayed. She understood that he didn't understand. So she stayed. I came to know her as she began to attend our church. After hearing her story, I asked what you would have asked. Why? Why didn't she give up? "Simple," she told me. "He's my brother."

Her pursuit reminds us of another, doesn't it? Another kind heart who left home in search of the confused. Another compassionate soul who couldn't bear the thought of a brother in pain. So, like Debbie, he left home. Like Debbie, he found his sibling.

And when God found us, we acted like Eric. We didn't recognize the one who came to help us. When he told us we were part of his family, we didn't believe him. When he offered a safe place to stay, we didn't follow him. We ignored him.

Some even cursed him and told him to leave.

But he didn't leave. He lingered. And still he lingers. He understands that we don't understand. He knows that we are torn by many voices and infected by a cancerous sin. He knows we are near death. But he doesn't want us to die alone.

Like Debbie, he wants to give us something before it's too late. He wants to give us a place in his family. And he wants to hold our hand when we die.

So God follows us. He pursues us along every roadside; he follows us down every highway. He follows us all the days of our lives. "Surely goodness and mercy shall follow me all the days of my life. And I will dwell in the house of the Lord forever" (Psalm 23:6).

What a surprising way to describe God. A God who pursues us.

Dare we envision a mobile, active God who chases us, tracks us, following us with goodness and mercy all the days of our lives? He's not hard to find. He's there in Scripture, looking for Adam and Eve. They're hiding in the bushes, partly to cover their bodies, partly to cover their sin. Does God wait for them to come to him? No, the words ring in the garden. "Where are you?" God asks (Genesis 3:9), beginning his quest to redeem the heart of man. A quest to follow his children until his children follow him.

Moses can tell you about it. After forty years in the desert, he looked over his shoulder and saw a bush blazing. God had followed him into the wilderness.

Jonah can tell you about it. He was a fugitive on a boat when he looked over his shoulder and saw clouds brewing. God had followed him onto the ocean.

The disciples of Jesus knew the feeling of being followed by God. They were rain-soaked and shivering when they looked over their shoulders and saw Jesus walking. God had followed them into the storm.

An unnamed Samaritan woman knew the same feeling. Alone in life and alone at the well, she looked over her shoulder and saw a Messiah speaking. God had followed her through her pain.

The apostle John, banished on Patmos, looked over his shoulder and saw the skies begin to open. God had followed him into his exile.

Lazarus had been dead for four days in a sealed tomb when a voice awakened him. He lifted his head and looked over his shoulder to see Jesus. God had followed him into death.

Peter the Apostle had denied his Lord and gone back to fishing when he heard his name and looked over his shoulder and saw Jesus cooking breakfast. God had followed him in spite of his failure.

Sin, wilderness, ocean, storm, pain, exile, death—our God is the God who follows. Have you sensed him following you? He is the one who came to seek and save the lost. Have you sensed him seeking you?

Have you felt his presence through the kindness of a stranger? Through the majesty of a sunset or the mystery of romance? Through the question of a child or the commitment of a spouse? Through a word well spoken or a touch well timed, have you sensed him?

Like Eric, we have left home. But, like Debbie, God has followed us. Like Eric, we are quick to turn away. But, like Debbie, God is slow to anger and determined to stay. We don't accept God's gifts. Yet God still gives them.

God gives us himself. Even when we choose our hovel over his house and our trash over his grace, still he follows. Never forcing us. Never leaving us. Patiently persistent. Faithfully present. He uses all his power to convince us that he is who he is and he can be trusted to lead us home.

By the way, Debbie's faithful persistence moved Eric's heart. Before his life ended, he acknowledged her as his sister. In doing so, he found his way home.

And that's what God wants for you. He simply wants you home with him. And to bring you home, he offers you a gift.

My prayer is that through these pages you'll see his gift like you've never seen it.

If you've already accepted it, you'll thank him again.

And if you've never accepted it, you will. For it's the gift of a lifetime, a gift for all people.

The Gift of a Savior

The Word became a human and lived among us.... The

Word was in the world and the world was made by him, but

the world did not know him.... But to all who did accept

him and believe in him he gave the right to become children

of God.... Because he was full of grace and truth, from him

we all received one gift after another.

JOHN 1:14, 10, 12, 16

IT WAS ABOUT TO BEGIN—GOD'S PLAN FOR HUMANITY,

CRAFTED IN THE HALLS OF HEAVEN AND CARRIED OUT

ON THE PLAINS OF EARTH. ONLY HOLINESS COULD HAVE

IMAGINED IT. ONLY DIVINITY COULD HAVE ENACTED IT.

ONLY RIGHTEOUSNESS COULD HAVE ENDURED IT. AND

ONCE THE PLAN BEGAN, THERE WOULD BE NO TURNING

BACK. THE CREATOR KNEW IT. THE SON KNEW IT.

AND SOON, EARTH ITSELF WOULD WITNESS HEAVEN'S

MAJESTY ALIGHTING ON THE PLANET.

IT BEGAN IN
A MANGER

*I*t all happened in a most remarkable moment...
a moment like no other. For through that segment of time a
spectacular thing occurred.

God became a man. Divinity arrived. Heaven opened herself
and placed her most precious one in a human womb.

The omnipotent, in one instant, became flesh and blood. The
one who was larger than the universe became a microscopic
embryo. And he who sustains the world with a word chose to be
dependent upon the nourishment of a young girl.

God had come near.

He came, not as a flash of light or as an unapproachable
conqueror, but as one whose first cries were heard by a peasant
girl and a sleepy carpenter. Mary and Joseph were anything but

royal. Yet heaven entrusted its greatest treasure to these simple parents. It began in a manger, this momentous moment in time. He looked anything but a king. His face, prunish and red. His cry, still the helpless and piercing cry of a dependent baby.

Majesty in the midst of the mundane. Holiness in the filth of sheep manure and sweat. This baby had overseen the universe. These rags keeping him warm were the robes of eternity. His golden throne room had been abandoned in favor of a dirty sheep pen. And worshiping angels had been replaced with kind but bewildered shepherds.

Curious, this royal throne room. No tapestries covering the windows. No velvet garments on the courtiers. No golden scepter or glittering crown. Curious, the sounds in the court. Cows munching, hooves crunching, a mother humming, a babe nursing.

It could have begun anywhere, the story of the king. But, curiously, it began in a manger. Step into the doorway, peek through the window.

He is here!

A DAY FOR GOOD-BYE

*I*t was time for Jesus to leave. The carpentry shop had been his home, his refuge. He had come to say good-bye, to smell the sawdust and lumber just one more time.

Life was peaceful here. Life was so safe. Here he had spent countless hours of contentment. On this dirt floor he had played as a toddler while his father worked. Here Joseph had taught him how to grip a hammer. And on this workbench he had built his first chair.

It was here that his human hands shaped the wood his divine hands had created. And it was here that his body matured while his spirit waited for the right moment, the right day.

And now that day had arrived.

I wonder if he wanted to stay.

I wonder because I know he had already read the last chapter. He knew that the feet that would step out of the safe shadow of the carpentry shop would not rest until they'd been pierced and placed on a Roman cross.

You see, he didn't have to go. He had a choice. He could have stayed. He could have ignored the call or at least postponed it. And had he chosen to stay, who would have known? Who would have blamed him?

He could have come back as a man in another era when society wasn't so volatile, when religion wasn't so stale, when people would listen better.

He could have come back when crosses were out of style.

But his heart wouldn't let him. If there was hesitation on the part of his humanity, it was overcome by the compassion of his divinity. His divinity heard the voices. His divinity heard the hopeless cries of the poor, the bitter accusations of the abandoned, the dangling despair of those who are trying to save themselves.

And his divinity saw the faces. Some wrinkled. Some weeping. Some hidden behind veils. Some obscured by fear. Some earnest with searching. Some blank with boredom. From the face of Adam to the face of the infant born somewhere in the world as you read these words, he saw them all.

And you can be sure of one thing. Among the voices that

found their way into that carpentry shop in Nazareth was your voice. Your silent prayers uttered on tearstained pillows were heard before they were said. Your deepest questions about death and eternity were answered before they were asked. And your direst need, your need for a Savior, was met before you ever sinned.

And not only did he hear you, he saw you. He saw your face aglow the hour you first knew him. He saw your face in shame the hour you first fell. The same face that looked back at you from this morning's mirror, looked at him. And it was enough to kill him.

He left because of you.

He laid his security down with his hammer. He hung tranquillity on the peg with his nail apron. He closed the window shutters on the sunshine of his youth and locked the door on the comfort and ease of anonymity.

Since he could bear your sins more easily than he could bear the thought of your hopelessness, he chose to leave.

It wasn't easy. But it was love.

GOD IN
THE FLESH

God chose to reveal himself through a human body.

The tongue that called forth the dead was a human one. The hand that touched the leper had dirt under its nails. The feet upon which the woman wept were calloused and dusty. And his tears…oh, don't miss the tears…they came from a heart as broken as yours or mine ever has been.

So, people came to him. My, how they came to him! They came at night; they touched him as he walked down the street; they followed him around the sea; they invited him into their homes and placed their children at his feet. Why? Because he refused to be a statue in a cathedral or a priest in an elevated pulpit. He chose instead to be a touchable, approachable, reachable Jesus.

There is not a hint of one person who was afraid to draw near him. There were those who mocked him. There were those who were envious of him. There were those who misunderstood him. There were those who revered him. But there was not one person who considered him too holy, too divine, or too celestial to touch. There was not one person who was reluctant to approach him for fear of being rejected.

COMPASSIONATE SAVIOR

They were like sheep without a shepherd.
So he began teaching them many things.

MARK 6:34

When Jesus landed and saw a large crowd, he had
compassion on them and healed their sick.

MATTHEW 14:14

*I*t's a good thing those verses weren't written about me.
It's a good thing thousands of people weren't depending on Max
for their teaching and nourishment. Especially on a day when I'd
just heard of the death of a dear friend. Especially on a day when
I wanted to be alone with my friends. Especially after I'd gotten
into a boat to escape the crowds. Had that been me in Jesus'

sandals on that Bethsaida beach, the verses would read something like:

> They were like sheep without a shepherd. So Max told them to quit grazing on his pasture and head back to their pens.
>
> When Max landed and saw a large crowd, he mumbled something about how hard it was to get a day off and radioed for the helicopter. Then he and the disciples escaped to a private retreat.

It's a good thing I wasn't responsible for those people. I would have been in no mood to teach them, no mood to help them. I would have had no desire even to be with them.

But, as I think about it, Jesus had no desire to be with them either. After all, he did leave them, didn't he? He had every intention of getting away and being alone. So what happened? Why didn't he tell them to get lost? What made him change his mind and spend the day with the people he was trying to avoid?

Answer? "He had *compassion* on them" (Matthew 14:14).

The Greek word for compassion is *splanchnizomai,* which won't mean much to you unless you are in the health professions and studied "splanchnology" in school. If so, you remember that "splanchnology" is a study of the visceral parts. Or, in contemporary jargon, a study of the gut.

When Matthew writes that Jesus had compassion on the people, he is not saying that Jesus felt casual pity for them. No, the term is far more graphic. Matthew is saying that Jesus felt their hurt in his gut:

> He felt the limp of the crippled.
> He felt the hurt of the diseased.
> He felt the loneliness of the leper.
> He felt the embarrassment of the sinful.

And once he felt their hurts, he couldn't help but heal their hurts. He was moved in the stomach by their needs. He was so touched by their needs that he forgot his own needs. He was so moved by the people's hurts that he put his hurts on the back burner. When Jesus arrived at Bethsaida, he was sorrowful, tired, and anxious to be alone with the disciples. No one would have blamed him had he dismissed the crowds a second time. No one would have criticized him had he waved away the people. But he didn't. Later he would. Later he would demand their departure and seek solitude.

But not before he "healed their sick" (Matthew 14:14) and taught them "many things" (Mark 6:34). Self was forgotten and others were served by the compassionate Savior.

JESUS KNOWS
HOW YOU FEEL

*J*esus knows how you feel. You're under the gun at work? Jesus knows how you feel. You've got more to do than is humanly possible? So did he. People take more from you than they give? Jesus understands. Your teenagers won't listen? Your students won't try? Jesus knows how you feel.

You are precious to him. So precious that he became like you so that you would come to him.

When you struggle, he listens. When you yearn, he responds. When you question, he hears. He has been there.

Like the little boy in the following story, Jesus sees you with a heart of compassion. He knows that you are special....

A boy went into a pet shop, looking for a puppy. The store owner showed him a litter in a box. The boy looked at the puppies. He picked each one up, examined it, and put it back in the box.

After several minutes, he walked back to the owner and said, "I picked one out. How much will it cost?"

The man gave him the price, and the boy promised to be back in a few days with the money. "Don't take too long," the owner cautioned. "Puppies like these sell quickly."

The boy turned and smiled knowingly. "I'm not worried," he said. "Mine will still be here."

The boy went to work—weeding, washing windows, cleaning yards. He worked hard and saved his money. When he had enough for the puppy, he returned to the store.

He walked up to the counter and laid down a pocketful of wadded bills. The store owner sorted and counted the cash. After verifying the amount, he smiled at the boy and said, "All right, son, you can go get your puppy."

The boy reached into the back of the box, pulled out a skinny dog with a limp leg, and started to leave.

The owner stopped him.

"Don't take that puppy," he objected. "He's crippled. He can't play. He'll never run with you. He can't fetch. Get one of the healthy pups."

"No, thank you, sir," the boy replied. "This is exactly the kind of dog I've been looking for."

As the boy turned to leave, the store owner started to speak but remained silent. Suddenly he understood. For extending from the bottom of the boy's trousers was a brace—a brace for his crippled leg.

Why did the boy want the dog? Because he knew how it felt. And he knew it was very special.

FAITH BEHELD,
FAITH BLESSED

A few days later, when Jesus came back to Capernaum, the news spread that he was at home. Many people gathered together so that there was no room in the house, not even outside the door. And Jesus was teaching them God's message. Four people came, carrying a paralyzed man. Since they could not get to Jesus because of the crowd, they dug a hole in the roof right above where he was speaking. When they got through, they lowered the mat with the paralyzed man on it. When Jesus saw the faith of these people, he said to the paralyzed man, "Young man, your sins are forgiven."

MARK 2:1-5

*J*esus was moved by this demonstration of faith. Four men had enough hope in him and love for their friend that they took a chance. The stretcher above was a sign from above—somebody believes! Someone was willing to risk embarrassment and injury for just a few moments with the Galilean.

Jesus was moved. So he applauds—if not with his hands, at least with his heart. And not only does he applaud, he blesses. And we witness a divine loveburst.

The friends want him to heal their friend. But Jesus won't settle for a simple healing of the body—he wants to heal the soul. He leapfrogs the physical and deals with the spiritual. To heal the body is temporal; to heal the soul is eternal.

The request of the friends is valid—but timid. The expectations of the crowd are high—but not high enough. They expect Jesus to say, "I heal you." Instead he says, "I forgive you." They expect him to treat the body, for that is what they see.

He chooses to treat not only the body, but also the spiritual, for that is what he sees.

They want Jesus to give the man a new body so he can walk. Jesus gives grace so the man can live.

Remarkable. Sometimes God is so touched by what he sees that he gives us what we need and not simply that for which we ask.

By the way, Jesus hasn't changed since the day a stretcher was lowered into his presence on the cords of hope.

What happened then still happens today. When we take a step of faith, God sees. The same face that beamed at the paralytic beams at the alcoholic refusing the bottle. The same eyes that danced at the friends dance at the mom and dad who will do whatever it takes to get their child to Jesus. And the same lips that spoke to the man in Capernaum speak to the man in Detroit, to the woman in Belfast, to the child in Moscow…to any person anywhere who dares to come into the presence of God and ask for help.

And though we can't hear it here, the angels can hear him there. All of heaven must pause as another burst of love declares the only words that really matter: "Your sins are forgiven."

THE GREAT
EXCHANGE

A friend of mine was at Disney World some time
back. He and his family sought a place to rest in Cinderella's
castle. Unfortunately, so did everyone else. The place was packed
with kids and parents. Suddenly all the children rushed to one
side. Had it been a boat, the castle would have tipped over.
Cinderella had entered.

Cinderella. The pristine princess. A gorgeous young girl with
each hair in place, flawless skin, and a beaming smile. She stood
waist-deep in a garden of kids, each wanting to touch and be
touched.

The other side of the castle was now vacant except for a boy
maybe seven or eight years old. His age was hard to determine
because of the disfigurement of his body. Dwarfed in height, face

deformed, he stood watching quietly and wistfully, holding the hand of an older brother.

Don't you know what he wanted? He wanted to be with the children. He longed to be in the middle of the kids reaching for Cinderella, calling her name. But can't you feel his fear, fear of yet another rejection? Fear of being taunted again, mocked again?

Don't you wish Cinderella would go to him? Guess what? She did!

She noticed the little boy. She immediately began walking in his direction. Politely but firmly inching through the crowd of children, she finally broke free. She walked quickly across the floor, knelt at eye level with the stunned little boy, and placed a kiss on his face.

The story reminds me of another royal figure. The names are different, but isn't the story almost the same? Rather than a princess of Disney, these essays are about the Prince of Peace. Rather than a boy in a castle, our story is about you and me. In both cases a gift was given. In both cases love was shared. In both cases the lovely one performed a gesture beyond words.

But Jesus did more than Cinderella. Oh, so much more. Cinderella gave only a kiss. When she stood to leave, she took her beauty with her. The boy was still deformed. What if Cinderella had done what Jesus did? What if she'd assumed his state? What if she had somehow given him her beauty and taken on his disfigurement?

That's what Jesus did.

"He took our suffering on him and felt our pain for us....He was wounded for the wrong we did; he was crushed for the evil we did. The punishment, which made us well, was given to him, and we are healed because of his wounds" (Isaiah 53:4–5).

Make no mistake:

Jesus gave more than a kiss—he gave his beauty.

He paid more than a visit—he paid for our mistakes.

He took more than a minute—he took away our sin.

EYES ON THE SAVIOR

A group of climbers set out to scale a large mountain in Europe. The view boasted a breathtaking peak of snowcapped rocks. On clear days the crested point reigned as king on the horizon. Its white tip jutted into the blue sky inviting admiration and offering inspiration.

On days like that the hikers made the greatest progress. The peak stood above them like a compelling goal. Eyes were called upward. The walk was brisk. The cooperation was unselfish. Though many, they climbed as one, all looking to the same summit.

Yet on some days the peak of the mountain was hidden from view. The cloud covering would eclipse the crisp blueness with a drab, gray ceiling and block the vision of the mountaintop. On those days the climb became arduous. Eyes were downward and thoughts inward. The goal was forgotten. Tempers were short. Weariness was an uninvited companion. Complaints stung like thorns on the trail.

We're like that, aren't we? As long as we can see our dream, as long as our goal is within eyesight, there is no mountain we can't climb or summit we can't scale. But take away our vision, block our view of the trail's end, and the result is as discouraging as the journey.

Think about it. Hide the Nazarene who calls to us from the mountaintop and see what happens.

Listen to the groans of the climbers as they stop and sit by the side of the path. Why continue if there is no relief in sight? Pilgrims with no vision of the promised land become proprietors of their own land. They set up camp. They exchange hiking boots for loafers and trade in their staffs for new recliners.

Instead of looking upward at him, they look inward at themselves and outward at each other. The result? Cabin fever. Quarreling families. Restless leaders. Fence-building. Staked-off territory. *No trespassing!* signs are hung on hearts and homes. Spats turn into fights as myopic groups turn to glare at each other's weaknesses instead of turning to worship their common Strength.

Mark it down. We are what we see. If we see only ourselves, our tombstones will have the same epitaph Paul used to describe enemies of Christ: "Their god is their own appetite, they glory in their shame, and this world is the limit of their horizon" (Philippians 3:19).

Humans were never meant to dwell in the stale fog of the lowlands with no vision of their Creator.

That's why God came near. To be seen.

And that's why those who saw him were never the same. "We saw his glory," exclaimed one follower.

"We were eyewitnesses of his majesty," whispered a martyr.

They saw the peak. They breathed the fresh air of the high country. They caught a glimpse of the pinnacle. And they refused to quit climbing until they reached the top. They wanted to see Jesus.

Seeing Jesus is what Christianity is all about. Christian service, in its purest form, is nothing more than imitating him who we see. To see his majesty and to imitate him, that is the sum of Christianity.

This is why those who see him today are never the same again.

Acquiring a vision of your Maker can be like starting a whole new life. It can be like a new birth. In fact, the One who inspired this book said that new beginnings and good eyesight are inseparable. "Unless a man is born again, he cannot see the kingdom of God."

If Jesus is who he says he is, there is no truth more worthy of your time and no god more worthy of your devotion. Keep climbing. And keep looking up. But make sure your eyes are on the Savior.

COME AND SEE

Nathanael said to Philip, "Can anything good come
from Nazareth?" Philip answered, "Come and see."

JOHN 1:46

*N*athanael's question still lingers, even two thousand
years later. Is the life of the young Nazarene really worth
considering?

The answer of Philip still suffices. "Come and see."

Come and see the rock that has withstood the winds of time.
Hear his voice.

The truth undaunted,

grace unspotted,

loyalty undeterred.

Come and see the flame that tyrants and despots have not extinguished.

Come and see the passion that oppression has not squelched.

Come and see the hospitals and orphanages rising beside the crumbling ruins of humanism and atheism. Come and see what Christ has done.

Can anything good come out of Nazareth? Come and see.

Come and see the changed lives:

> the alcoholic now dry,

>> the embittered now joyful,

>>> the shamed now forgiven.

Come and see the marriages rebuilt, the orphans embraced, the imprisoned inspired.

Journey into the jungles and hear the drums beating in praise.

Sneak into the corners of communism and find believers worshiping under threat of death.

Walk on death row and witness the prisoner condemned by man yet liberated by God.

Can anything good come out of Nazareth?

Come and see the pierced hand of God touch the most common heart, wipe the tear from the wrinkled face, and forgive the ugliest sin.

Come and see. He avoids no seeker. He ignores no probe. He

fears no search. Come and see. Nathanael came. And Nathanael saw. And Nathanael discovered: "Teacher, you are the Son of God; you are the King of Israel."

Ransom for Sinners

But God showed his great love for us in this way: Christ

died for us while we were still sinners.

ROMANS 5:8

JESUS, DO YOU GIVE NO THOUGHT TO SAVING

YOURSELF? WHAT KEEPS YOU THERE? WHAT HOLDS

YOU TO THE CROSS? NAILS DON'T HOLD GODS TO

TREES. WHAT MAKES YOU STAY?

ROAD TO CALVARY

*C*hrist came to earth for one reason: to give his life as a ransom for you, for me, for all of us. He sacrificed himself to give us a second chance. He would have gone to any lengths to do so. And he did. He went to the cross, where man's utter despair collided with God's unbending grace. And in that moment when God's great gift was complete, the compassionate Christ showed the world the cost of his gift.

Trace the path of this Savior, the God who swapped heavenly royalty for earthly poverty. His bed became, at best, a borrowed pallet—and usually the hard earth. He was dependent on handouts for his income. He was sometimes so hungry he would eat raw grain or pick fruit off a tree. He knew what it meant to have no home. He was ridiculed. His neighbors tried to lynch him. Some called him a lunatic. His family tried to confine him to their house. His friends weren't always faithful to him.

He was accused of a crime he never committed. Witnesses were hired to lie. The jury was rigged. A judge swayed by politics handed down the death penalty.

They killed him.

And why? Because of the gift that only he could give.

He who was perfect gave that perfect record to us, and our imperfect record was given to him. Jesus was "not guilty, but he suffered for those who are guilty to bring you to God" (1 Peter 3:18). As a result, God's holiness is honored and his children are forgiven.

THE FOG OF A
BROKEN HEART

They went to a place called Gethsemane, and Jesus
said to his disciples, "Sit here while I pray." He took
Peter, James and John along with him, and he began
to be deeply distressed and troubled. Horror and
dismay came over him, and he said to them, "My
heart is ready to break with grief; stop here, and stay
awake." Then he went forward a little, threw himself
on the ground, and prayed that, if it were possible,
this hour might pass him by. "Abba, Father," he said,
"all things are possible to thee; take this cup away
from me. Yet not what I will, but what you will."

MARK 14:32-36

*L*ook at those phrases. "*Horror* and *dismay* came over him." "My heart is ready to *break* with grief." "He went forward a little and *threw* himself on the ground."

Does this look like the picture of a saintly Jesus resting in the palm of God? Hardly. Mark used black paint to describe this scene. We see an agonizing, straining, and struggling Jesus. We see a "man of sorrows." We see a man struggling with fear, wrestling with commitments, and yearning for relief.

We see Jesus in the fog of a broken heart.

The writer of Hebrews would later pen, "During the days of Jesus' life on earth, he offered up prayers and petitions with *loud cries and tears* to the one who could save him from death" (Hebrews 5:7).

My, what a portrait! Jesus is in pain. Jesus is on the stage of fear. Jesus is cloaked, not in sainthood, but in humanity.

The next time the fog finds you, you might do well to remember Jesus in the garden. The next time you think that no one understands, reread the fourteenth chapter of Mark. The next time your self-pity convinces you that no one cares, pay a visit to Gethsemane. And the next time you wonder if God really perceives the pain that prevails on this dusty planet, listen to him pleading among the twisted trees.

Seeing God like this does wonders for our own suffering. God was never more human than at this hour. God was never nearer to us than when he hurt. The Incarnation was never so fulfilled as in the garden.

As a result, time spent in the fog of pain could be God's greatest gift. It could be the hour that we finally see our Maker. If it is true that in suffering God is most like man, maybe in our suffering we can see God like never before.

Watch closely. It could very well be that the hand that extends itself to lead you out of the fog is a pierced one.

PARTNER
IN THE PLAN

Jesus was given to you, and with the help of those who don't know the law, you put him to death by nailing him to a cross. But this was God's plan which he had made long ago; he knew this would happen. God raised Jesus from the dead and set him free from the pain of death, because death could not hold him.

ACTS 2:23–24

The cross was no accident.

Jesus' death was not the result of a panicking cosmological engineer. The cross wasn't a tragic surprise. Calvary was not a knee-jerk response to a world plummeting toward destruction. It wasn't a patch-up job or a stop-gap measure. The death of the Son of God was anything but an unexpected peril.

No, it was part of an incredible plan. A calculated choice.

The moment the forbidden fruit touched the lips of Eve, the shadow of a cross appeared on the horizon. And between that moment and the moment the man with the mallet placed the spike against the wrist of God, a master plan was fulfilled.

What does that mean? It means Jesus planned his own sacrifice.

It means Jesus intentionally planted the tree from which his cross would be carved.

It means he willingly placed the iron ore in the heart of the earth from which the nails would be cast.

It means he voluntarily placed his Judas in the womb of a woman.

It means Christ was the one who set in motion the political machinery that would send Pilate to Jerusalem.

And it also means he didn't have to do it—but he did.

It was no accident—would that it had been! Even the cruelest of criminals is spared the agony of having his death sentence read to him before his life even begins.

But Jesus was born crucified. Whenever he became conscious of who he was, he also became conscious of what he had to do. The cross-shaped shadow could always be seen. And the screams of hell's imprisoned could always be heard.

This explains the glint of determination on his face as he

turned to go to Jerusalem for the last time. He was on his death march (Luke 9:51).

This explains the resoluteness in the words, "The reason my Father loves me is that I lay down my life—only to take it up again. No one takes it from me, but I lay it down of my own accord" (John 10:17–18).

The cross explains why John the Baptist introduced Jesus to the crowds as the "Lamb of God, who takes away the sin of the world!" (John 1:29).

Maybe it's why he tore the grass out by the roots in Gethsemane. He knew the hell he'd endure for saying, "Thy will be done."

Maybe the cross was why he so loved children. They represented the very thing he would have to give: Life.

The ropes used to tie his hands and the soldiers used to lead him to the cross were unnecessary. They were incidental. Had they not been there, had there been no trial, no Pilate, and no crowd, the very same crucifixion would have occurred. Had Jesus been forced to nail himself to the cross, he would have done it. For it was not the soldiers who killed him, nor the screams of the mob: It was his devotion to us.

So call it what you wish: An act of grace. A plan of redemption. A martyr's sacrifice. But whatever you call it, don't call it an accident. It was anything but that.

HE SAW YOU

*T*he final prayer of Jesus was about you. His final pain was for you. His final passion was for you. Before he went to the cross, Jesus went to the garden. And when he spoke with his Father, you were in his prayers. As Jesus looked into heaven, you were in his vision. As Jesus dreamed of the day when we will be where he is, he saw you there....

Never had he felt so alone. What had to be done, only he could do. An angel couldn't do it. No angel has the power to break open hell's gates. A man couldn't do it. No man has the purity to destroy sin's claim. No force on earth can face the force of evil and win—except God.

And God couldn't turn his back on you. He couldn't because he saw you, and one look at you was all it took to convince him.

Right there in the middle of a world which isn't fair. He saw you cast into a river of life you didn't request. He saw you betrayed by those you love. He saw you with a body which gets sick and a heart which grows weak.

He saw you in your own garden of gnarled trees and sleeping friends. He saw you staring into the pit of your own failures and the mouth of your own grave. He saw you in your Garden of Gethsemane—and he didn't want you to be alone.

He wanted you to know that he has been there, too. He knows what it's like to be plotted against. He knows what it's like to be confused. He knows what it's like to be torn between two desires. He knows what it's like to smell the stench of Satan. And, perhaps most of all, he knows what it's like to beg God to change his mind and to hear God say so gently, but firmly, "No."

For that is what God said to Jesus. And Jesus accepted the answer. At some moment during that midnight hour an angel of mercy came over the weary body of the man in the garden. Jesus stood, the anguish gone from his eyes. His heart will fight no more.

The battle has been won. The sign of conquest? Jesus at peace in the olive trees.

On the eve of the cross, Jesus made his decision. He would rather go to hell for you than go to heaven without you.

HEAVEN'S SILENCE

During the darkest night of his life, Jesus experienced unanswered prayer, unfruitful service, and unbelievable betrayal. Jesus had just offered an anguished appeal to God. "My Father, if it is possible, do not give me this cup of suffering. But do what you want, not what I want" (Matthew 26:39). Matthew says that Jesus was "very sad and troubled" (Matthew 26:37). The Master "fell to the ground" (Matthew 26:39) and cried out to God. Luke tells us that Jesus was "full of pain" and that "his sweat was like drops of blood falling to the ground" (Luke 22:44).

Never has earth offered such an urgent request. And never has heaven offered more deafening silence. The prayer of Jesus was unanswered. *Jesus* and *unanswered prayer* in the same phrase? Isn't that an oxymoron? Would the son of Henry have no Ford or the child of Bill Gates own no computer? Would God, the one who owns the cattle on a thousand hills, keep something from his own Son? He did that night. And that was just the beginning. Look who showed up next:

Judas arrived with an angry crowd (Matthew 26:47, 51). Not only did Jesus have to face unanswered prayer, he also had to deal with unfruitful service. The very people he came to save had now come to arrest him.

Unbelievable betrayal: *All* pledged loyalty, and yet *all* ran. The disciples have left him. Unfruitful service: The people have rejected him. And, perhaps most hurtful: unanswered prayer. God hasn't heard him. From a human point of view, Jesus' world has collapsed. No answer from heaven, no help from the people, no loyalty from his friends.

Yet somehow, despite all the pain, Jesus was able to see good in the bad, the purpose in the pain, and God's presence in the problem.

He found good in the bad. It would be hard to find someone worse than Judas. The Bible says, "Judas...was a thief. He was the one who kept the money box, and he often stole from it" (John 12:6). Somehow Judas was able to live in the presence of God and experience the miracles of Christ and remain unchanged. In the end he decided he'd rather have money than a friend, so he sold Jesus for thirty pieces of silver. Judas was a scoundrel, a cheat, and a bum. How could anyone see him any other way?

Somehow Jesus did. Only inches from the face of his betrayer, Jesus looked at him and said, "Friend, do what you came to do" (Matthew 26:50). What Jesus saw in Judas as worthy of being called a friend, I can't imagine. But I do know that Jesus doesn't lie, and in that moment he saw something good in a very bad man.

Not only did Jesus find good in the bad, he found purpose in the pain. Of the ninety-eight words Jesus spoke at his arrest, thirty refer to the purpose of God. "It must happen this way to bring about what the Scriptures say" (v. 54). "All these things have happened so that it will come about as the prophets wrote" (v. 56).

Jesus chose to see his immediate struggle as a necessary part of a greater plan. He viewed the Gethsemane conflict as an important but singular act in the grand manuscript of God's drama.

Where we see unanswered prayer, Jesus saw answered prayer. Where we see the absence of God, Jesus saw the plan of God. Note especially verse 53: "Surely you know I could ask my Father, and he would give me more than twelve armies of angels."

Jesus saw what mattered. He saw his Father. He saw his Father's presence in the problem.

AT ANY COST

God on a cross. The ultimate act of creative compassion. The Creator being sacrificed for the creation. God convincing man once and for all that he would give anything, pay any price to save his children. He could have given up. He could have turned his back. He could have walked away from the wretched mess the world became, but he didn't.

God didn't give up.

When people from his own hometown tried to push him over a cliff, he didn't give up.

When his brothers ridiculed him, he didn't give up.

When he was accused of blaspheming God by people who didn't fear God, he didn't give up.

When Peter worshiped him at the supper and cursed him at the fire, he didn't give up.

When people spat in his face, he didn't spit back. When the bystanders slapped him, he didn't slap them. When a whip ripped his sides, he didn't turn and command the awaiting angels to stuff that whip down that soldier's throat.

And when human hands fastened the divine hands to a cross with spikes, it wasn't the soldiers who held the hands of Jesus steady. It was God who held them steady. Those same hands that formed the oceans and built the mountains. Those same hands that designed the dawn and crafted each cloud. Those same hands that blueprinted one incredible plan for you and me.

Take a stroll out to the hill. Out to Calvary. Out to the cross where, with holy blood, the hand that placed you on the planet wrote the promise, "God would give up his only Son before he'd give up on you."

RIGHT OR RIGHTEOUS?

*I*t wasn't right that people spit into the eyes that had wept for them. It wasn't right that soldiers ripped chunks of flesh out of the back of their God. It wasn't right that spikes pierced the hands that formed the earth. And it wasn't right that the Son of God was forced to hear the silence of God.

It wasn't right, but it happened.

For while Jesus was on the cross, God sat on his hands. He turned his back. He ignored the screams of the innocent.

He sat in silence while the sins of the world were placed upon his Son. And he did nothing while a cry a million times bloodier than John's echoed in the black sky: "My God, my God, why have you forsaken me?"

Was it right? No.

Was it fair? No.

Was it love? Yes.

In a world of injustice, God once and for all tipped the scales in the favor of hope. And he did it by sitting on his hands so that we could know the kingdom of God.

HEARTBROKEN
FOR YOU

*I*t was the most gut-wrenching cry of loneliness in history, and it came not from a prisoner or a widow or a patient. It came from a hill, from a cross, from a Messiah.

"My God, my God!" he screamed. "Why did you abandon me!"

Never have words carried so much hurt. Never has one being been so lonely.

The despair is darker than the sky. The two who have been one are now two. Jesus, who had been with God for eternity, is now alone. The Christ, who was an expression of God, is abandoned. The Trinity is dismantled. The Godhead is disjointed. The unity is dissolved.

It is more than Jesus can take. He withstood the beatings and remained strong at the mock trials. He watched in silence as those he loved ran away. He did not retaliate when the insults were hurled nor did he scream when the nails pierced his wrists.

But when God turned his head, that was more than he could handle.

"My God!" The wail rises from parched lips. The holy heart is broken. The Sinbearer screams as he wanders in the eternal wasteland. Out of the silent sky come the words screamed by all who walk in the desert of loneliness. "Why? Why did you abandon me?"

I can't understand it. I honestly cannot. Why did Jesus do it? Oh, I know, I know. I have heard the official answers. "To gratify the old law." "To fulfill prophecy." And these answers are right. They are. But there is something more here. Something very compassionate. Something yearning. Something personal.

What is it?

Could it be that his heart was broken for all the people who cast despairing eyes toward the dark heavens and cry the same "Why?" Could it be that his heart was broken for the hurting? Could it be his desire to take on their pain propelled him to the cross? If he could have, wouldn't he have run to the cross on behalf of all the pain in the world?

I imagine him, bending close to those who hurt. I imagine him listening. I picture his eyes misting and a pierced hand brushing away a tear. And although he may offer no answer, although he may solve no dilemma, although the question may freeze painfully in midair, he who also was once alone, understands.

"IT IS FINISHED!"

*A*re any words in history more splendid? Three words, at once shattering and victorious.

"It is finished."

Stop and listen a moment. Let the words wind through your heart. Imagine the cry from the cross. The sky is dark. The other two victims are moaning. Jeering mouths of the crowd are silent. Perhaps there is thunder. Perhaps there is weeping. Perhaps there is silence. Then Jesus draws in a deep breath, pushes his feet down on that Roman nail, and cries, "It is finished!"

What was finished?

The history-long plan of redeeming man was finished. The message of God to man was finished. The works done by Jesus as a man on earth were finished. The task of selecting and training ambassadors was finished. The job was finished. The song had been sung. The blood had been poured. The sacrifice had been made. The sting of death had been removed. It was over.

A cry of defeat? Hardly. Had his hands not been fastened down I dare say that a triumphant fist would have punched the dark sky. No, this is no cry of despair. It is a cry of completion. A cry of relief. A roar of fulfillment. A shout of victory.

"Father!" (The voice is hoarse.)
The voice that called forth the dead,
the voice that taught the willing,
the voice that screamed at God,
now says, "Father!"
"Father."

It's over.
An angel sighs. A star wipes away a tear.

"Take me home."
Yes, take him home.
Take this prince to his king.
Take this Son to his Father.
Take this pilgrim to his home.
    (He deserves a rest.)
"Take me home."

Come, ten thousand angels! Come and take this
    wounded Troubadour to
        the cradle of his Father's arms!

Farewell, manger's infant.
Bless you, holy ambassador.
Go home, death slayer.
Rest well, sweet soldier.
    The battle is over.

Bounteous Grace

God showed his love for us in this way: Christ died for us while

we were still sinners.

ROMANS 5:8

And you never again have to wonder who your father is—

you've been adopted by God and are therefore an "heir of God

through Christ."

GALATIANS 4:7

PONDER THE ACHIEVEMENT OF GOD. HE DOESN'T

CONDONE OUR SIN, NOR DOES HE COMPROMISE HIS

STANDARD. HE DOESN'T IGNORE OUR REBELLION, NOR

DOES HE RELAX HIS DEMANDS. RATHER THAN DISMISS

OUR SIN, HE ASSUMES OUR SIN AND, INCREDIBLY,

SENTENCES HIMSELF. GOD'S HOLINESS IS HONORED. OUR

SIN IS PUNISHED...AND WE ARE REDEEMED. GOD DOES

WHAT WE CANNOT DO SO WE CAN BE WHAT WE DARE

NOT DREAM: PERFECT BEFORE GOD.

GRACIOUS PROMISES

Therefore, there is now no condemnation for those who are in Christ Jesus.

ROMANS 8:1

[God] justifies those who have faith in Jesus.

ROMANS 3:26

For I will forgive their wickedness and will remember their sins no more.

HEBREWS 8:12

*F*or those in Christ, these promises are not only a source of joy. They are also the foundations of true courage. You are guaranteed that your sins will be filtered through, hidden in, and screened out by the sacrifice of Jesus. When God looks at you, he doesn't see you; he sees the One who surrounds you. That means that failure is not a concern for you. Your victory is secure. How could you not be courageous?

Picture it this way. Imagine that you are an ice-skater in competition. You are in first place with one more round to go. If you perform well, the trophy is yours. You are nervous, anxious, and frightened.

Then, only minutes before your performance, your trainer rushes to you with the thrilling news: "You've already won! The judges tabulated the scores, and the person in second place can't catch you. You are too far ahead."

Answer the big question of eternity, and the little questions of life fall into perspective.

PARDON AND PEACE

Through Christ's sacrifice, our past is pardoned and our future secure. And, "Since we have been made right with God by our faith, we have peace with God" Romans 5:1.

Peace with God. What a happy consequence of faith! Not just peace between countries, peace between neighbors, or peace at home; salvation brings peace with God.

Once a monk and his apprentice traveled from the abbey to a nearby village. The two parted at the city gates, agreeing to meet the next morning after completing their tasks. According to plan, they met and began the long walk back to the abbey. The monk noticed that the younger man was unusually quiet. He asked him if anything was wrong. "What business is it of yours?" came the terse response.

Now the monk was sure that his brother was troubled, but he said nothing. The distance between the two began to increase. The apprentice walked slowly, as if to separate himself from his teacher. When the abbey came in sight, the monk stopped at the gate and waited for the student. "Tell me, my son. What troubles your soul?"

The boy started to react again, but when he saw the warmth in his master's eyes, his heart began to melt. "I have sinned greatly," he sobbed. "Last night I slept with a woman and abandoned my vows. I am not worthy to enter the abbey at your side."

The teacher put his arm around the student and said, "We will enter the abbey together. And we will enter the cathedral together. And together we will confess your sin. No one but God will know which of the two of us fell."

Doesn't that describe what God has done for us? When we kept our sin silent, we withdrew from him. We saw him as an enemy. We took steps to avoid his presence. But our confession of fault alters our perception. God is no longer a foe, but a friend. We are at peace with him. He did more than the monk did, much more. More than share in our sin, Jesus was "crushed for the evil we did. The punishment which made us well was given to him" (Isaiah 53:5). "He accepted the shame" (Hebrews 12:2). He leads us into the presence of God.

GRASPING GRACE

*L*ord, if it's you," Peter says, "tell me to come to you on the water" (Matthew 14:28).

Peter is not testing Jesus; he is pleading with Jesus. Stepping onto a stormy sea is not a move of logic; it is a move of desperation. Peter grabs the edge of the boat. Throws out a leg...follows with the other. Several steps are taken. It's as if an invisible ridge of rocks runs beneath his feet. At the end of the ridge is the glowing face of a never-say-die friend.

We do the same, don't we? We come to Christ in an hour of deep need. We abandon the boat of good works. We realize, like Moses, that human strength won't save us. So we look to God in desperation. We realize, like Paul, that all the good works in the world are puny when laid before the Perfect One. We realize, like Peter, that spanning the gap between us and Jesus is a feat too great for our feet.

So we beg for help. Hear his voice. And step out in fear, hoping that our little faith will be enough.

Faith is not born at the negotiating table where we barter our gifts in exchange for God's goodness. Faith is not an award given to the most learned. It's not a prize given to the most disciplined. It's not a title bequeathed to the most religious.

Faith is a desperate dive out of the sinking boat of human effort and a prayer that God will be there to pull us out of the water. The apostle Paul wrote about this kind of faith:

"For it is by grace you have been saved, through faith—and this not from yourselves, it is the gift of God—not by works, so that no one can boast" (Ephesians 2:8–9).

The supreme force in salvation is God's grace. Not our works. Not our talents. Not our feelings. Not our strength.

Grace is God's sudden, calming presence during the stormy seas of our lives. We hear his voice; we take the step. Why? Because we are great sinners and we need a great Savior.

We, like Peter, are aware of two facts: We are going down and God is standing up. So we scramble out. We leave behind the Titanic of self-righteousness and stand on the solid path of God's grace.

And, surprisingly, we are able to walk on water. Death is disarmed. Failures are forgivable. Life has real purpose. And God is not only within sight, he is within reach.

GRACE MEANS...

*H*ere's a secret about grace—ten little words that explain all you need to know: "If God is for us, who can be against us?" (Romans 8:31). That's really all you need to know. And while it sounds simple, there's a profound message contained within those ten words.

Let's take a look at four words in this verse that deserve your attention. Read slowly the phrase, "God is for us." Please pause for a minute before you continue. Read it again, aloud. *God is for us.* Repeat the phrase four times, this time emphasizing each word. (Come on, you're not in that big of a hurry.)

God is for us.

God *is* for us.

God is *for* us.

God is for *us.*

God is for you. Your parents may have forgotten you, your teachers may have neglected you, your siblings may be ashamed of you; but within reach of your prayers is the maker of the oceans. God!

God *is* for you. Not "may be," not "has been," not "was," not "would be," but "God is!" He is for you. Today. At this hour. At this minute. As you read this sentence. No need to wait in line or come back tomorrow. He is with you. He could not be closer than he is at this second. His loyalty won't increase if you are better nor lessen if you are worse. He is for you.

God is *for* you. Turn to the sidelines; that's God cheering your run. Look past the finish line; that's God applauding your steps. Listen for him in the bleachers, shouting your name. Too tired to continue? He'll carry you. Too discouraged to fight? He's picking you up. God is for you.

God is for *you*. Had he a calendar, your birthday would be circled. If he drove a car, your name would be on his bumper. If there's a tree in heaven, he's carved your name in the bark. We know he has a tattoo, and we know what it says. "I have written your name on my hand," he declares (Isaiah 49:16).

"Can a mother forget the baby at her breast and have no compassion on the child she has borne?" God asks (Isaiah 49:15). What a bizarre question. Can you mothers imagine feeding your infant and then later asking, "What was that baby's name?" No.

I've seen you care for your young. You stroke the hair, you touch the face, you sing the name over and over. Can a mother forget? No way. But "even if she could forget…I will not forget you," God pledges (Isaiah 49:15).

God is for you. Knowing that, who is against you? Can death harm you now? Can disease rob your life? Can your purpose be taken or your value diminished? No. Though hell may set itself against you, no one can defeat you. You are protected. God is for you.

And that's what grace means.

WITH TOWEL
AND BASIN

It was almost time for the Jewish Passover Feast. Jesus
knew that it was time for him to leave this world and
go back to the Father. He had always loved those who
were his own in the world, and he loved them all the
way to the end.... So during the meal Jesus stood
up...poured water into a bowl and began to wash the
followers' feet.

JOHN 13:1-5

*B*ehold the gift Jesus gives his followers! He knows
what these men are about to do. He knows they are about to
perform the vilest act of their lives. By morning they will bury
their heads in shame and look down at their feet in disgust. And

when they do, he wants them to remember how his knees knelt before them and he washed their feet. He wants them to realize those feet are still clean.

Remarkable. He forgave their sin before they even committed it. He offered mercy before they even sought it. Aside from geography and chronology, our story is the same as the disciples'. We weren't in Jerusalem, and we weren't alive that night. But what Jesus did for them he has done for us. He has cleansed us. He has cleansed our hearts from sin.

Even more, he is still cleansing us! "We are being cleansed from every sin by the blood of Jesus" (1 John 1:7). In other words, we are always being cleansed. The cleansing is not a promise for the future but a reality in the present. Let a speck of dust fall on the soul of a saint, and it is washed away. Let a spot of filth land on the heart of God's child, and the filth is wiped away. Jesus still cleans his disciples' feet. Jesus still washes away stains. Jesus still purifies his people.

Our Savior kneels down and gazes upon the darkest acts of our lives. But rather than recoil in horror, he reaches out in kindness and says, "I can clean that if you want." And from the basin of his grace, he scoops a palm full of mercy and washes our sin.

ADOPTION
OF THE HEART

amily therapist Paul Faulkner tells of the man who set out to adopt a troubled teenage girl. One would question his logic. She was destructive, disobedient, and dishonest.

One day she came home from school and ransacked the house looking for money. By the time he arrived, she was gone and the house was in shambles.

Upon hearing of her actions, a friend urged him not to finalize the adoption. "You haven't completed the paperwork. You haven't signed any documents. Let her go."

His response was simply, "But I've already promised her that she would be my daughter."

God, too, has made a covenant to adopt his people. His covenant is not invalidated by our rebellion. It's one thing to love us when we are strong, obedient, and willing. But when we ransack his house and steal what is his? This is the test of love.

And God passes the test. "For God shows his great love for us in this way: Christ died for us while we were still sinners" (Romans 5:8).

The father didn't look at the wrecked house and say, "Come back when you've learned respect."

God didn't look at our frazzled lives and say, "I'll die for you when you deserve it."

No, despite our sin, in the face of our rebellion, he chose to adopt us. And for God, there's no going back. His grace is a come-as-you-are promise from a one-of-a-kind King. You've been found, called, and adopted; so trust your Father and claim this verse as your own: "God showed his love for us in this way: Christ died for us while we were still sinners" (Romans 5:8). And you never again have to wonder who your father is—you've been adopted by God and are therefore an "heir of God through Christ" (Galatians 4:7).

THE SOURCE
OF MY STRENGTH

*D*uring the early days of the Civil War a Union soldier was arrested on charges of desertion. Unable to prove his innocence, he was condemned and sentenced to die a deserter's death. His appeal found its way to the desk of Abraham Lincoln. The president felt mercy for the soldier and signed a pardon. The soldier returned to service, fought the entirety of the war, and was killed in the last battle. Found within his breast pocket was the signed letter of the president.

Close to the heart of the soldier were his leader's words of pardon. He found courage in grace. I wonder how many thousands more have found courage in the emblazoned cross of their heavenly king.

If you need a bit of courage, let me show you a source of

strength for your journey. Keep these words close to your heart and be confident that, because of grace:

- ✦ You are beyond condemnation (Romans 8:1).
- ✦ You are delivered from the law (Romans 7:6).
- ✦ You are near God (Ephesians 2:13).
- ✦ You are delivered from the power of evil (Colossians 1:13).
- ✦ You are a member of his kingdom (Colossians 1:13).
- ✦ You are justified (Romans 5:1).
- ✦ You are perfect (Hebrews 10:14).
- ✦ You have been adopted (Romans 8:15).
- ✦ You have access to God at any moment (Ephesians 2:18).
- ✦ You are a part of his priesthood (1 Peter 2:5).
- ✦ You will never be abandoned (Hebrews 13:5).
- ✦ You have an imperishable inheritance (1 Peter 1:4).
- ✦ You are a partner with Christ in life (Colossians 3:4), privilege (Ephesians 2:6), suffering (2 Timothy 2:12), and service (1 Corinthians 1:9).

And know that in the heart of God, you are a:

- ✦ member of his body (1 Corinthians 12:13).
- ✦ branch in the vine (John 15:5).
- ✦ stone in the building (Ephesians 2:19–22).

+ bride for the groom (Ephesians 5:25–27).
+ saint in the new generation (1 Peter 2:9).
+ dwelling place of the Spirit (1 Corinthians 6:19).

You possess (get this!) every spiritual blessing possible. "In Christ, God has given us every spiritual blessing in the heavenly world" (Ephesians 1:3). This is the gift offered to the lowliest sinner on earth. Who could make such an offer but God? "From him we have all received one gift after another" (John 1:16).

> Everything comes from him;
> Everything comes through him;
> Everything ends up in him.
> Always glory! Always praise! Yes. Yes. Yes.
>
> ROMANS 11:33–36

The Choice

And being found in appearance as a man, [Jesus] humbled

himself and became obedient to death—even death on a

cross! Therefore God exalted him to the highest place and

gave him the name that is above every name, that at the

name of Jesus every knee should bow, in heaven and on

earth and under the earth, and every tongue confess that

Jesus Christ is Lord, to the glory of God the Father.

PHILIPPIANS 2:8–11

ON ONE SIDE STANDS THE CROWD.

JEERING. BAITING. DEMANDING.

ON THE OTHER STANDS A PEASANT.

SWOLLEN LIPS. LUMPY EYE. LOFTY PROMISE.

ONE PROMISES ACCEPTANCE, THE OTHER A CROSS.

ONE OFFERS FLESH AND FLASH, THE OTHER OFFERS FAITH.

THE CROWD CHALLENGES, "FOLLOW US AND FIT IN."

JESUS PROMISES, "FOLLOW ME AND STAND OUT."

THEY PROMISE TO PLEASE. GOD PROMISES TO SAVE.

A BASIN OF WATER? OR THE BLOOD OF THE SAVIOR?

GOD LOOKS AT YOU AND ASKS...

WHICH WILL BE YOUR CHOICE?

THE GOD
WHO INVITES

od is an inviting God. He invited Mary to birth his
son, the disciples to fish for men, the adulteress woman
to start over, and Thomas to touch his wounds. God is the King
who prepares the palace, sets the table, and invites his subjects to
come in.

In fact, it seems his favorite word is *come*.

"*Come,* let us talk about these things. Though your sins are
like scarlet, they can be as white as snow."

"All you who are thirsty, *come* and drink."

"*Come* to me all, all of you who are tired and have heavy
loads, and I will give you rest."

"*Come* to the wedding feast."

"*Come* follow me, and I will make you fish for people."

"Let anyone who is thirsty *come* to me and drink."

God is a God who invites. God is a God who calls. God is a God who opens the door and waves his hand, pointing pilgrims to a full table.

His invitation is not just for a meal, however; it is for life. An invitation to come into his kingdom and take up residence in a tearless, graveless, painless world. Who can come? Whoever wishes. The invitation is at once universal and personal.

To know God is to receive his invitation. Not just to hear it, not just to study it, not just to acknowledge it, but to receive it. It is possible to learn much about God's invitation and never respond to it personally.

Yet his invitation is clear and nonnegotiable. He gives all and we give him all. Simple and absolute. He is clear in what he asks and clear in what he offers. The choice is up to us. Isn't it incredible that God leaves the choice to us? Think about it. There are many things in life we can't choose. We can't, for example, choose the weather. We can't control the economy.

We can't choose whether or not we are born with a big nose or blue eyes or a lot of hair. We can't even choose how people respond to us.

But we can choose where we spend eternity. The big choice, God leaves to us. The critical decision is ours.

That is the only decision which really matters. Whether or

not you take the job transfer is not critical. Whether or not you buy a new car is not crucial. What college you choose or what profession you select is important, but not compared to where you spend eternity. That is the decision you will remember. It is the choice of a lifetime.

LEAVING THE PORCH LIGHT ON

He's waiting for you. God is standing on the porch of heaven, expectantly hoping, searching the horizon for a glimpse of his child. You're the one God is seeking.

God is the waiting Father, the caring Shepherd in search of his lamb. His legs are scratched, his feet are sore, and his eyes are burning. He scales the cliffs and traverses the fields. He explores the caves. He cups his hands to his mouth and calls into the canyon.

And the name he calls is yours.

He is the Housewife in search of the lost coin. No matter that he has nine others; he won't rest until he has found the tenth. He searches the house. He moves furniture. He pulls up rugs. He cleans out the shelves. All other tasks can wait. Only one matters—the coin of great value to him. He owns it. He will not stop until he finds it.

The coin he seeks is you.

God is the Father pacing the porch. His eyes are wide with his quest. His heart is heavy. He seeks his prodigal. He searches the horizon, yearning for the familiar figure, the recognizable gait. His concern is the son who wears his name, the child who bears his image. You.

He wants you home.

God wants you to be free of yesterday's guilt. He wants you free of today's fears. He wants you free of tomorrow's grave. Sin, fear, and death. These are the mountains he has moved by the power of the cross. These are the prayers he will answer through the gift of his love.

The message is simple: God gave up his Son in order to rescue all his sons and daughters. To bring his children home. He's listening for your answer.

TOO GOOD
TO BE TRUE?

hen does salvation come? When we look to Christ. When we embrace him as Savior. Astonishingly simple, isn't it? Claim the great promise of John 3:16: "God loved the world so much that he gave his one and only Son so that whoever believes in him may not be lost, but have eternal life."

God, the Lover. God, the Giver. God, the Savior.

And man, the believer. And for those who believe, he has promised a new birth.

But despite the simplicity, there are still those who don't believe. They don't trust the promise. They can't imagine how God could forgive their sins. It's almost too good to be true.

If only they would try. If only they would test it. But God is as polite as he is passionate. He never forces his way in. The choice is theirs.

And for those who do come, he has promised a new birth.

Does that mean the old nature will never rear its ugly head? Does that mean you will instantly be able to resist any temptation?

To answer that question, compare your new birth in Christ to a newborn baby. Can a newborn walk? Can he feed himself? Can he sing or read or speak? No, not yet. But someday he will.

It takes time to grow. But is the parent in the delivery room ashamed of the baby? Is the mom embarrassed that the infant can't spell…that the baby can't walk…that the newborn can't give a speech?

Of course not. The parents aren't ashamed; they are proud. They know that growth will come with time. So does God. "God is being patient with you. He does not want anyone to be lost, but he wants all people to change their hearts and lives" (2 Peter 3:9).

God is often more patient with us than we are with ourselves. We assume that if we fall, we aren't born again. If we stumble, then we aren't truly converted. If we have the old desires, then we must not be a new creation.

Please remember: "God began doing a good work in you, and I am sure he will continue it until it is finished when Jesus Christ comes again" (Philippians 1:6).

In many ways, your new birth in Christ is like your first: In your new birth, God provides what you need and someone else does the work. And just as parents are patient with their newborn, so God is patient with you. But there is one difference. The first time you had no choice about being born; this time you do. The power is God's. The effort is God's. The pain is God's.

But the choice is yours.

WHO'S TO CHOOSE?

To whom does God offer his gift? To the brightest? The most beautiful or the most charming? No. His gift is for us all—beggars and bankers, clergy and clerks, judges and janitors. All God's children.

And he wants us so badly, he'll take us in any condition—"as is" reads the tag on our collars. He's not about to wait for us to reach perfection (he knows we'll never get there!). Do you think he's waiting for us to overcome all temptations? Hardly. When we master the Christian walk? Far from it. Remember, Christ died for us when we were still sinners. His sacrifice, then, was not dependent on our performance.

He wants us *now*. And he'll do whatever it takes to bring his children home.

Christ's love has no strings, no expectations, no hidden agendas, no secrets. His love for us is up front and clear. "I love you," he says. "Even if you let me down. I love you in spite of your failures."

Why did God choose you? Why did he choose me? Honestly. Why? What do we have that he needs?

Intellect? Do we honestly think for one minute that we have—or ever will have—a thought he hasn't had?

Willpower? I can respect that. Some of us are stubborn enough to walk on water if we felt called to do so…but to think God's kingdom would have done a belly-up without our determination?

Beauty, talent, charm? Right. All those came from him in the first place. Why then? Why would he choose you?

The answer is at once simple and profound. He chose you because he wanted to. After all, you are his. He made you. He brought you home. He owns you. And if you've never heard him assuring you of that simple fact, be reminded by the words on this page. Let these words resonate in your heart: the God who created you loves you. He made the ultimate sacrifice because of *you*. No, God doesn't need you. He *wants* you. So, what do we do with this gift? What does it have to do with our daily existence?

It has *everything* to do with it. Our task on earth is

singular—to choose our eternal home. You can afford many wrong choices in life. You can choose the wrong career and survive, the wrong city and survive, the wrong house and survive. You can even choose the wrong mate and survive. But there is one choice that must be made correctly and that is your eternal destiny.

PURSUED BY GOD

*H*ow far do you want God to go in getting your attention? If God has to choose between your eternal safety and your earthly comfort, which do you hope he chooses?

What if he moved you to another land? (As he did Abraham.) What if he called you out of retirement? (Remember Moses?) How about the voice of an angel or the bowel of a fish? (À la Gideon and Jonah.) How about a promotion like Daniel's or a demotion like Samson's?

God does what it takes to get our attention. Isn't that the message of the Bible? The relentless pursuit of God. God on the hunt. God in the search. Peeking under the bed for hiding kids, stirring the bushes for lost sheep. Cupping hand to mouth and shouting into the canyon. Wrestling with us Jacobs in the muddy Jabboks of life.

For all its peculiarities and unevenness, the Bible has a simple story. God made man. Man rejected God. God won't give up until he wins him back. From Moses in Moab to John on Patmos, God is as creative as he is relentless. The same hand that sent manna to Israel sent Uzzah to his death. The same hand that set the children free from Israel also sent them captive to Babylon. Both kind and stern. Tender and tough. Faithfully firm. Patiently urgent. Eagerly tolerant. Softly shouting.

God's voice gently thundering, "I want you."

And your response?

Jesus said, "I am the bread that gives life. I am the light of the world. I am the resurrection and the life. I am the door. I am the way, the truth, and the life. I will come back and take you with me" (John 6:48; 8:12; 11:25; 10:9; 14:6; 14:3).

Jesus proclaiming—ever offering but never forcing: Standing over the crippled man: "Do you want to be well?" (John 5:6).

Eye to eye with the blind man, now healed: "Do you believe in the Son of Man?" (John 9:35).

Near the tomb of Lazarus, probing the heart of Martha: "Everyone who lives and believes in me will never die. Martha, do you believe this?" (John 11:26).

Honest questions. Thundering claims. Gentle touch. Never going where not invited, but once invited never stopping until he's finished, until a choice has been made.

God will whisper. He will shout. He will touch and tug. He will take away our burdens; he'll even take away our blessings. If there are a thousand steps between us and him, he will take all but one. But he will leave the final one for us.

The choice is ours.

A DEMONSTRATION
OF DEVOTION

*D*oes this sound like you? You have nothing to give God but problems. All you have to offer him is your hurt. You want to accept his gift of grace, but you feel unworthy of his sacrifice.

Maybe that has kept you from coming to God. Oh, you've taken a step or two in his direction. But then you saw the other people who follow him. They seemed so clean, so neat, so trim and fit in their faith. So you hesitated.

If that description fits, read the story of the nameless woman in Mark 5. She, considered unclean by her culture, demonstrated her devotion to Jesus by touching the hem of the Savior's garment. And that slight gesture moved Jesus to heal her. She was a shame-struck, penniless outcast who clutched onto her hunch that he could and her hope that he would.

Isn't that what faith is all about? A conviction that he can and that he will. Sounds similar to the definition of faith given by the Bible: "Without faith no one can please God. Anyone who comes to God must believe that he is real and that he rewards those who truly want to find him" (Hebrews 11:6).

Not too complicated, is it? Faith is the belief that God is real and that God is good. Faith is not a mystical experience or a midnight vision or a voice in the forest...it is a choice to believe that the One who made it all hasn't left it all and that he still sends light into shadows and responds to gestures of faith.

Faith is not the belief that God will do what you want. Faith is the belief that God will do what is right. God is always near and always available. Just waiting for your touch. So let him know. Demonstrate your devotion:

Write a letter.

Ask forgiveness.

Confess.

Be baptized.

Feed a hungry person.

Pray.

Teach.

Go.

Do something that reveals your faith. For faith with no effort is no faith at all. God will respond. He has never rejected a genuine gesture of faith. Never.

God honors radical, risk-taking faith. When arks are built, lives are saved. When soldiers march, Jerichos tumble. When staffs are raised, seas still open. When a lunch is shared, thousands are fed. And when a garment is touched—whether by the hand of an anemic woman in Galilee or by the prayers of a beggar in Bangladesh—Jesus stops. So make your choice, announce your faith to God, and demonstrate your devotion.

YOUR ABBA'S ARMS

*S*ome time back, my daughter Jenna and I spent several days in the old city of Jerusalem. One afternoon, as we were exiting the Jaffa gate, we found ourselves behind an Orthodox Jewish family—a father and his three small girls.

One of the daughters, perhaps four or five years of age, fell a few steps behind and couldn't see her father.

"*Abba!*" she called to him. He stopped and looked. Only then did he realize he was separated from his daughter.

"*Abba!*" she called again. He spotted her and immediately extended his hand. She took it and I took mental notes as they continued. I wanted to see the actions of an *abba*.

He held her hand tightly in his as they descended the ramp. When he stopped at a busy street, she stepped off the curb, so he pulled her back. When the signal changed, he led her and her sisters through the intersection. In the middle of the street, he reached down and swung her up into his arms and continued their journey.

Isn't that what we all need? An *abba* who will hear when we call? Who will take our hand when we're weak? Who will guide us through the hectic intersections of life? Don't we all need an *abba* who will swing us up into his arms and carry us home? We all need a father.

There's a God in heaven who wants you to call him your *abba*.

Choosing God as Lord is to acknowledge that he is sovereign and supreme in the universe. To accept him as Savior is to accept his gift of salvation offered on the cross. But to regard him as Abba—Father—is to go one step further. Ideally, a father is the one in your life who provides and protects. That is exactly what God has done.

He has provided for your needs (Matthew 6:25–34). He has protected you from harm (Psalm 139:5). He has adopted you (Ephesians 1:5). And he has given you his name (1 John 3:1).

God has proven himself as a faithful father. Now it falls to us to be trusting children. Let God give you what the world cannot. Rely on him alone for your affirmation and encouragement. Hold onto these glorious words: "You are God's child, and God will give you the blessing he promised, because you are his child" (Galatians 4:7).

Turn to God. Your abba is waiting for you, with arms open wide.

GOD'S DESTINY
FOR YOUR LIFE

I can remember, as a seven-year-old, going to my grandparents' house for a week. Mom and Dad bought a ticket, gave me some spending money, put me on a Greyhound bus, and told me not to talk to strangers or get off the bus until I saw my grandma out the window. They made it very clear to me that my destination was Ralls, Texas.

God has done the same for you. He has placed you on a journey. He has a destiny for your life (and you'll be glad to know it's not Ralls, Texas).

> For God has not destined us for wrath,
> but to obtain salvation through our Lord Jesus.
>
> 1 THESSALONIANS 5:9

According to the Bible, God's destiny for your life is salvation. Your intended destination is heaven. God has done exactly what my parents did. He has purchased our passage. He has equipped us for the journey. God loves you so much that he wants you to be with him forever.

The choice, however, is up to you. Even though he stands at the door with ticket paid and pocket money for the trip, many choose to go in other directions than the one God intends. That is our problem.

OUR PROBLEM: SIN *(We're on the wrong bus.)*

When my parents gave me the ticket and told me which bus to board, I believed them and did what they said. I trusted them. I knew they loved me and I knew they knew more than I did...so I got on board.

Becoming a Christian is getting on board with Christ. Jesus stands at the door of the bus and says, "I am the way, the truth, and the life. No one comes to the Father but by me" (John 14:6). Unfortunately, not all accept his invitation. I know I didn't the first time he invited. I spent some time on the wrong bus.

There are many buses, each of them promising to take you to happiness. There are the buses of pleasure, possessions, power, passion. I saw a bus called party and got on board. It was full of people laughing and carousing; they seemed to be enjoying a nonstop party. It was quite some time before I learned they had to be loud to cover up all the pain inside.

The word for getting on the wrong bus is *sin*. Sin is when we say, "I'll go my way instead of God's way." Right in the middle of the word *sin* is the word *I*. Sin is when we say, *I'll do what I want, no matter what God says*. Only God can fulfill our needs. Sin is the act of going to everyone but God for what only God can give. Am I the only one who has spent time on the wrong bus? No. Some buses are more violent than others. Some rides are more lengthy than others, but:

> All of us, like sheep, have gone astray, and
> each of us has turned to his own way.
>
> ISAIAH 53:6
>
> If we say we never sin, we are only fooling
> ourselves, and refuse to accept the truth.
>
> 1 JOHN 1:8
>
> We're sinners, every one of us in the same
> sinking boat with everyone else.
>
> ROMANS 3:20

To board the wrong bus is a serious mistake. Sin breaks our relationship with God. We were intended to journey with him. But when we are on a different bus headed the wrong direction, we feel far from God. This is why life can seem so cruddy. We aren't fulfilling our destiny.

Sin not only breaks our relationship with God; it hampers our relationship with others. Can you imagine taking a long trip to the wrong place with a busload of people? With time, everyone gets cranky. Nobody likes the trip. The journey is miserable.

We try to cope with the problems by therapy or recreation or prescriptions. But nothing helps. The Bible says:

> There are ways that seem right to a man, but they only end in death.
>
> PROVERBS 16:25

You see, the end result of sin is death…spiritual death. "The wages of sin," Paul writes, "is death…" (Romans 6:23). Spend a lifetime on the wrong bus headed in the wrong direction and you'll end up in the wrong place. You'll end up in hell. Not because God wants you in hell. His plan for you is heaven. Your destiny is heaven. He'll do anything to get you to heaven, with one exception. There is one thing he won't do. He won't force you. The decision is yours. But he has done everything else. Let me show you what I mean.

THE SOLUTION: GRACE *(Go to the right bus.)*

If the problem is sin and all have sinned, what can I do? Well, you can go to church, but that won't make you a Christian. Just as going to a rodeo doesn't make you a cowboy, going to church doesn't make you a Christian. You could work hard to please God. You could do a lot of good stuff, give away a lot of things…the only problem with that is that you don't know how many good things you have to do. Or you could compare yourself with others. "I may be bad, but at least I'm better than Hitler." The problem with comparisons is that other people aren't the standard; God is!

So what are you going to do? If you aren't saved by going to church or doing good works or comparing yourself to others, how are you saved? The answer is simple: go to the right bus.

> For God so loved the world that he gave
> his one and only Son, that whoever believes in him
> shall not perish but have eternal life.
>
> JOHN 3:16

Note what God did: "He gave his only Son." This is how he dealt with your sin. Imagine it this way: Suppose you are found guilty of a crime. You are in a courtroom in front of the judge and he sentences you to death for your crime. His sentence is just. You are guilty and the punishment for your crime is death. But suppose that the judge is your father. He knows the law; he knows that your crime demands a death. But he knows love; he knows that he loves you too much to let you die. So in a wonderful act of love he steps down from the bench and removes his robe and stands by your side and says, "I'm going to die in your place."

That is what God did for you. The wages of sin is death. Heaven's justice demands a death for your sin. Heaven's love, however, can't bear to see you die. So here is what God did. He stood and removed his heavenly robes. He came to earth to tell us that he would die for us. He would be our Savior. And that is what he did.

> God put the world square with himself through the Messiah, giving the world a fresh start by offering the forgiveness of sins…God put on him the wrong who never did anything wrong, so we could be put right with God.
>
> 2 CORINTHIANS 5:21

THE RESPONSE: TRUST *(Getting on the right bus.)*

What does God want you to do? He wants you to get on his bus. How is this done? Three simple steps: admit, agree, accept.

1. Admit that God has not been first place in your life and ask him to forgive your sins.

   If we confess our sins, he is faithful and just and will forgive our sins and cleanse us from every wrong.

   1 JOHN 1:9

2. Agree that Jesus died to pay for your sins and that he rose from the dead and is alive today.

   If you confess that Jesus is your Lord, and you believe in your heart that God raised him from the dead, you will be saved.

   ROMANS 10:9

   Salvation is found in no one else, for there is no other name [Jesus] by which we must be saved.

   ACTS 4:12

3. Accept God's free gift of salvation. Don't try to earn it.

   For it is by grace that you have been saved, through faith—and this is not from yourselves, it is the gift of God—not by works, so that no one can boast.

   EPHESIANS 2:8-9

   To all who received him, he gave the right to become children of God. All they needed to do was to trust him to save them. All those who believe this are reborn!—not a physical rebirth...but from the will of God.

JOHN 1:12-13

Jesus says, Listen, I stand at the door and knock. If anyone hears my voice and opens the door, I will come in...

REVELATION 3:20

With all of my heart, I urge you to accept God's destiny for your life. I urge you to get on board with Christ. According to the Bible, "Jesus is the only one who can save people. His name is the only power in the world that has been given to save people. We must be saved through him" (Acts 4:12).

Would you let him save you? This is the most important decision you will ever make. Why don't you give your heart to him right now? *Admit* your need. *Agree* with his work. *Accept* his gift. Go to God in prayer and tell him, "I am a sinner in need of grace. I believe that Jesus died for me on the cross. I accept your offer of salvation." It's a simple prayer with eternal results.

Once you've placed your faith in Christ, I urge you to take three steps. You'll find them easy to remember. Just think of these three words (they each start with *b*): baptism, Bible, and belong.

Baptism demonstrates and celebrates our decision to follow

Jesus. Our immersion into water symbolizes our immersion into God's grace. Just as water cleanses the body, so grace cleanses the soul. Jesus said, "Anyone who believes and is baptized will be saved" (Mark 16:16). When the apostle Paul became a believer, he was asked this question: "Now, why wait any longer? Get up, be baptized, and wash your sins away, trusting in him to save you" (Acts 22:16). Paul responded by being baptized immediately. You can, too.

Bible reading brings us face-to-face with God. God reveals himself to us through his Word by the Holy Spirit. "Let the teaching of Christ live in you richly" (Colossians 3:16).

Belonging to a church reinforces your faith. A Christian without a church is like a baseball player without a team or a soldier without an army. You aren't strong enough to survive alone. "You should not stay away from the church meetings as some are in the habit of doing, but you should meet together and encourage each other" (Hebrews 10:25).

These three steps—baptism, Bible reading, and belonging to a church—are essential steps in your faith.

I pray that you'll accept this great gift of salvation. Believe me, this is not only the most important decision you'll ever make; it's the greatest decision you'll ever make. There's no higher treasure than God's gift of salvation. It's God's wonderful destiny for your life.

✦

REFERENCES

"It Began in a Manger" is taken from *God Came Near* (Sisters, OR: Multnomah Publishers, Inc., 1987).

"A Day for Good-bye" is taken from *God Came Near* (Sisters, OR: Multnomah Publishers, Inc., 1987).

"God in the Flesh" is taken from *God Came Near* (Sisters, OR: Multnomah Publishers, Inc., 1987).

"Compassionate Savior" is taken from *In the Eye of the Storm* (Nashville, TN: Word Publishing, 1991).

"Jesus Knows How You Feel" is taken from *In the Eye of the Storm* (Nashville, TN: Word Publishing, 1991).

"Faith Beheld, Faith Blessed" is taken from *He Still Moves Stones* (Nashville, TN: Word Publishing, 1993).

"The Great Exchange" is taken from *A Gentle Thunder* (Nashville, TN: Word Publishing, 1995).

"Eyes on the Savior" is taken from *God Came Near* (Sisters, OR: Multnomah Publishers, Inc., 1987).

"Come and See" is taken from *A Gentle Thunder* (Nashville, TN: Word Publishing, 1995).

"Road to Calvary" is taken from *The Applause of Heaven* (Nashville, TN: Word Publishing, 1990).

"The Fog of a Broken Heart" is taken from *No Wonder They Call Him the Savior* (Sisters, OR: Multnomah Publishers, Inc., 1986).

"Partner in the Plan" is taken from *God Came Near* (Sisters, OR: Multnomah Publishers, Inc., 1987).

"He Saw You" is taken from *And the Angels Were Silent* (Sisters, OR: Multnomah Publishers, Inc., 1992).

"Heaven's Silence" is taken from *Just Like Jesus* (Nashville, TN: Word Publishing, 1998).

"At Any Cost" is taken from *Six Hours One Friday* (Sisters, OR: Multnomah Publishers, Inc., 1989).

"Right or Righteous?" is taken from *The Applause of Heaven* (Nashville, TN: Word Publishing, 1990).

"Heartbroken for You" is taken from *No Wonder They Call Him the Savior* (Sisters, OR: Multnomah Publishers, Inc., 1986).

"It Is Finished!" is taken from *No Wonder They Call Him the Savior* (Sisters, OR: Multnomah Publishers, Inc., 1986).

Introduction to "Bounteous Grace" is taken from *In the Grip of Grace* (Nashville, TN: Word Publishing, 1996).

"Gracious Promises" is taken from *The Applause of Heaven* (Nashville, TN: Word Publishing, 1990).

"Pardon and Peace" is taken from *In the Grip of Grace* (Nashville, TN: Word Publishing, 1996).

"Grasping Grace" is taken from *In the Eye of the Storm* (Nashville, TN: Word Publishing, 1991).

"Grace Means…" is taken from *In the Grip of Grace* (Nashville, TN: Word Publishing, 1996).

"With Towel and Basin" is taken from *Just Like Jesus* (Nashville, TN: Word Publishing, 1998)

"Adoption of the Heart" is taken from *In the Grip of Grace* (Nashville, TN: Word Publishing, 1996).

"The Source of My Strength" is taken from *In the Grip of Grace* (Nashville, TN: Word Publishing, 1996).

"The God Who Invites" is taken from *And the Angels Were Silent* (Sisters, OR: Multnomah Publishers, Inc., 1992).

"Leaving the Porch Light On" is taken from *And the Angels Were Silent* (Sisters, OR: Multnomah Publishers, Inc., 1992).

"Too Good to Be True?" is taken from *A Gentle Thunder* (Nashville, TN: Word Publishing, 1995).

"Who's to Choose?" is taken from *No Wonder They Call Him the Savior* (Sisters, OR: Multnomah Publishers, Inc., 1986), 156, and *And the Angels Were Silent* (Sisters, OR.: Multnomah Publishers, Inc., 1992).

"Pursued by God" is taken from *A Gentle Thunder* (Nashville, TN: Word Publishing, 1995).

"A Demonstration of Devotion" is taken from *He Still Moves Stones* (Nashville, TN: Word Publishing, 1993).

"Your Abba's Arms" is taken from *The Great House of God* (Nashville, Tenn.: Word Publishing, 1993), 136–137, and *He Still Moves Stones* (Nashville, TN: Word Publishing, 1993).